Easy to Read! • Easy to Draw!

Animals

For the kids at Gatewood Elementary School—JH

ISBN: 0-8431-4548-X   A B C D E F G H I J

Easy to Read! • Easy to Draw!

Animals

By Joan Holub

Illustrated by
Joan Holub and Dana Regan

PSS!
PRICE STERN SLOAN

I can draw animals
that bark, oink, and meow.
You can draw them, too.
I'll show you how.

I can draw my dog.

Use these shapes to draw a dog.

1.

2.

3.

4.

5.

6.

7.

8. Now draw a bone.

I can draw my cat.

Use these shapes to draw a cat.

1.

2.

3.

4.

5.

6.

7.

8. Now draw a mouse.

I can draw a bird.

Use these shapes to draw a bird.

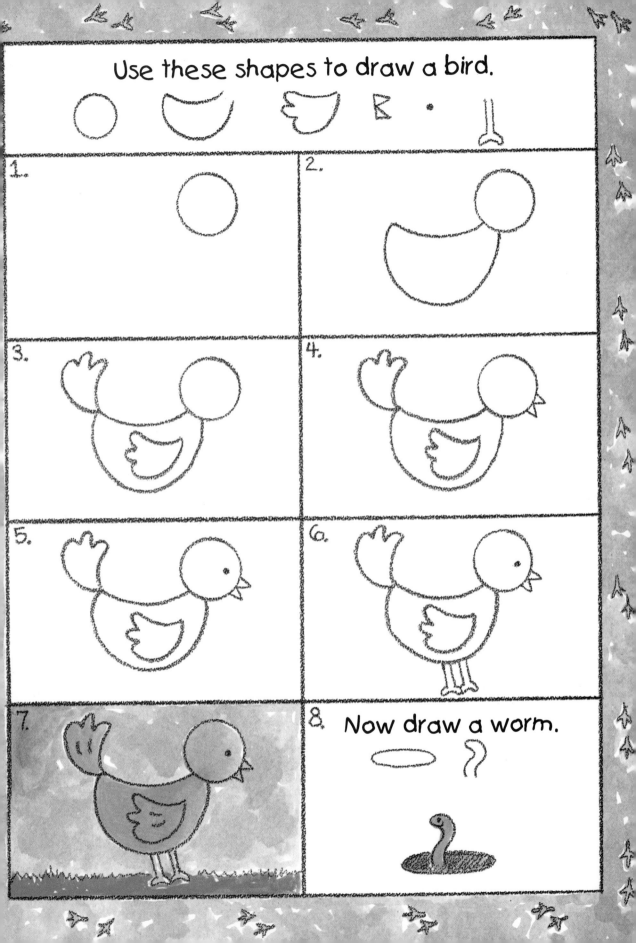

1.

2.

3.

4.

5.

6.

7.

8. Now draw a worm.

I can draw a bat.

Use these shapes to draw a bat.

I like to draw animals.
I want to draw more!
Let's go look for animals
at the pet store!

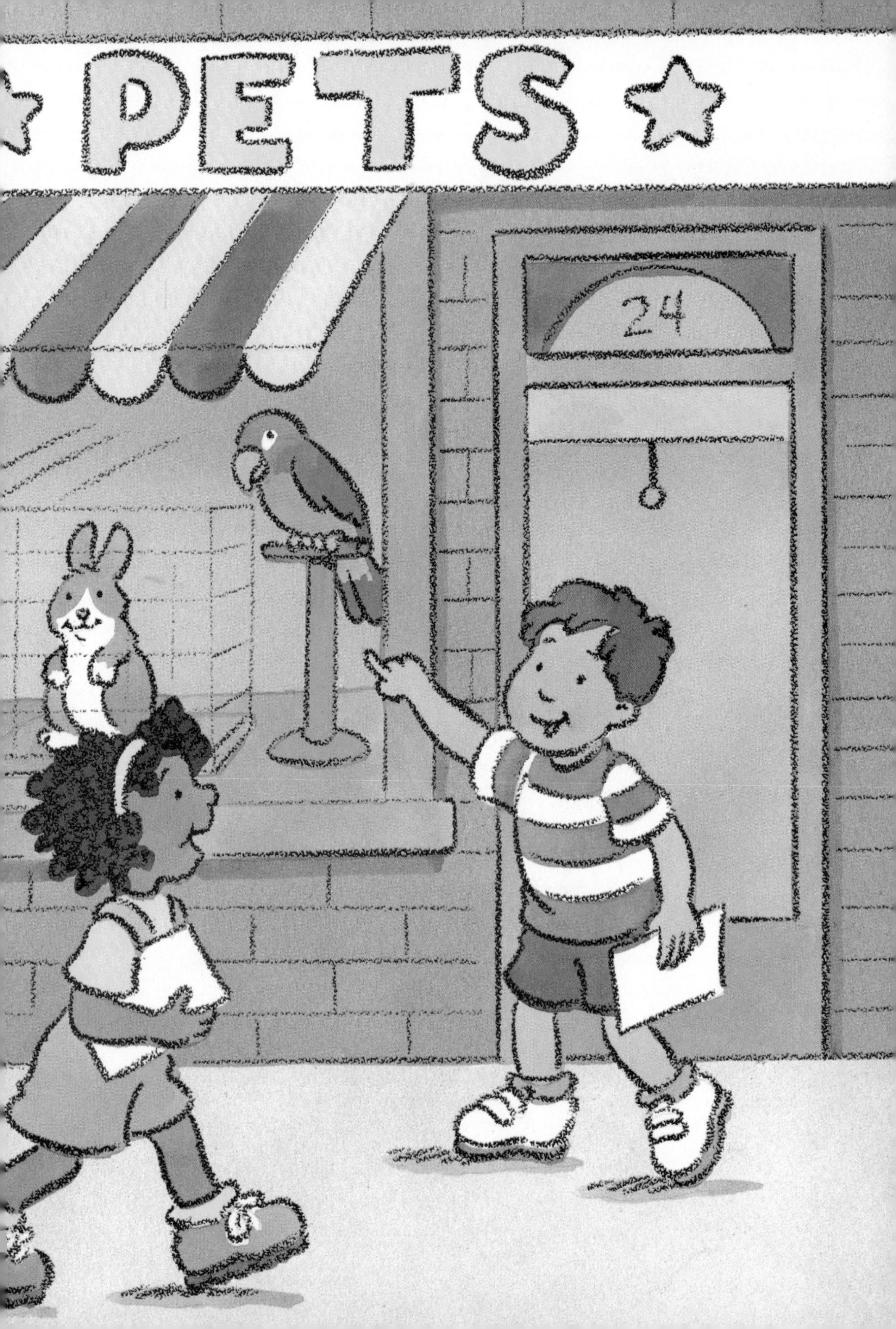
PETS
24

I can draw a hamster.

Use these shapes to draw a hamster.

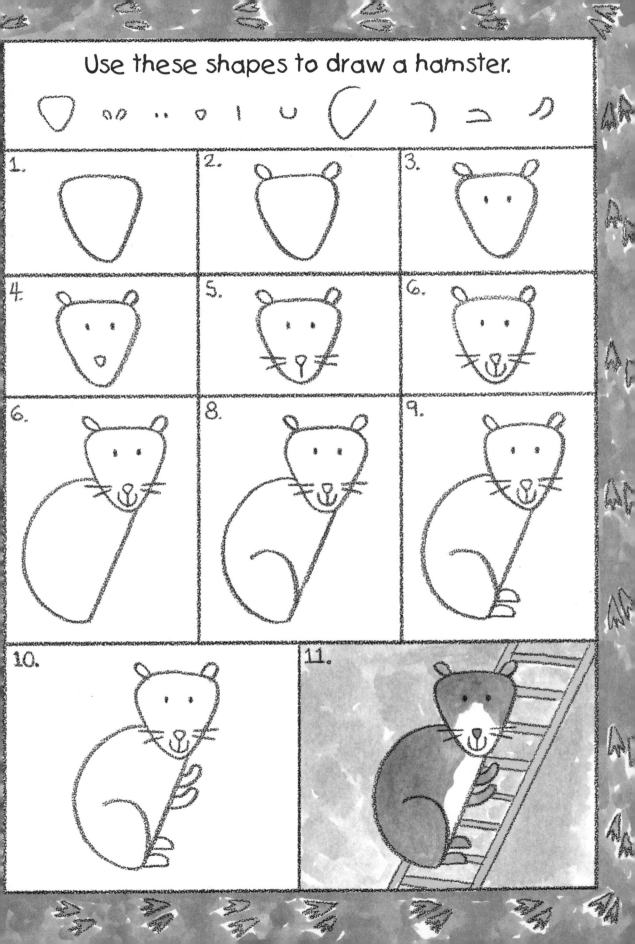

I can draw a snake.

Use these shapes to draw a snake.

1.

2.

3.

4.

5.

6.

7.

8.

9.

Oops! I can erase
when I make a mistake.

I can draw a rabbit
that goes hop, hop.
I like to draw.
I don't want to stop.

Use these shapes to draw a rabbit.

1.

2.

3.

4.

5.

6.

7.

8. Now draw a carrot.

I can draw animals.
I've drawn quite a few.
Now I'll draw animals
that live in the zoo.

I can draw a lion
that roars at me.

Use these shapes to draw a lion.

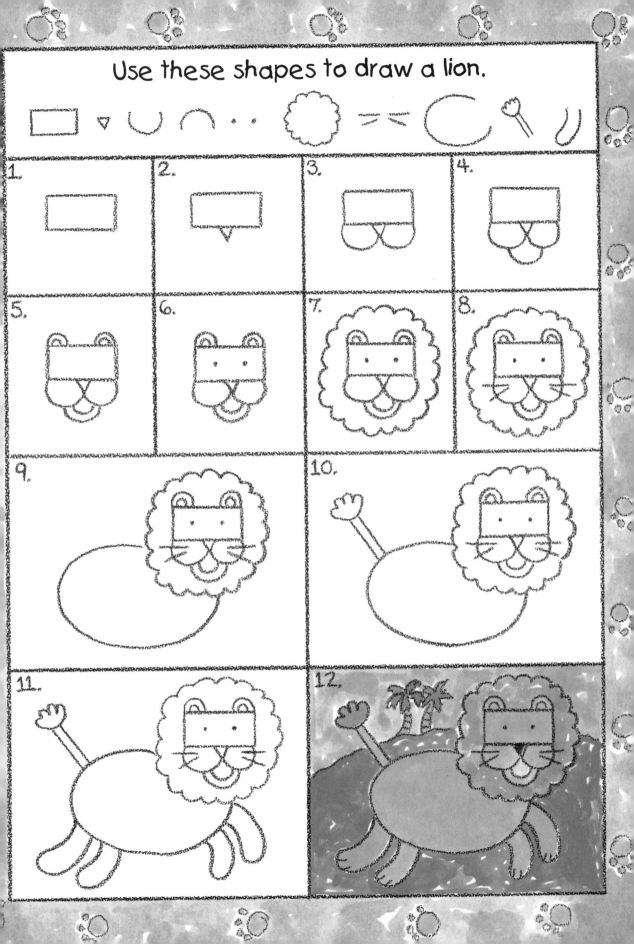

I can draw a monkey
that swings in a tree.

Use these shapes to draw a monkey.

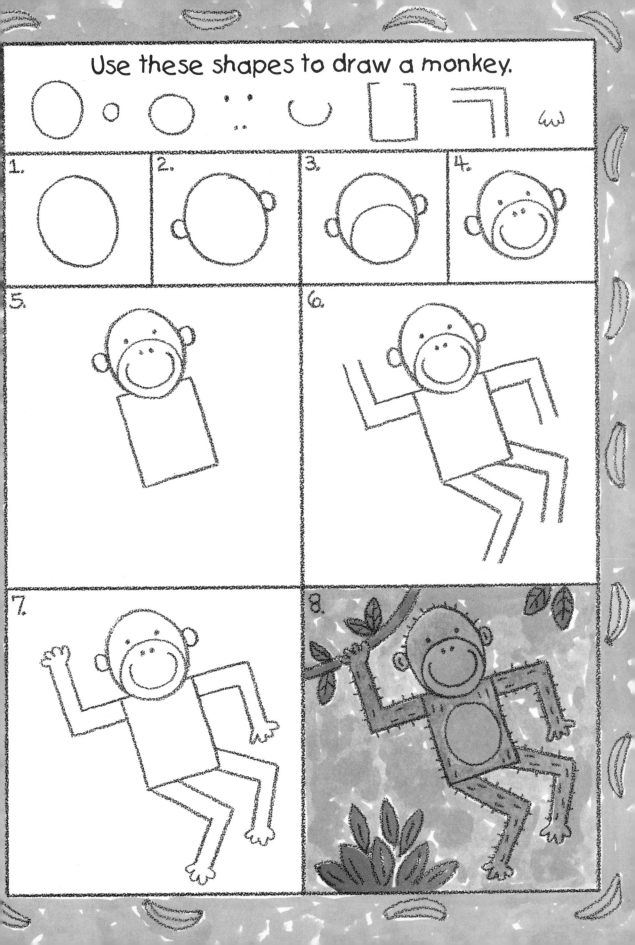

I can draw an elephant,
and that isn't all.

Use these shapes to draw an elephant.

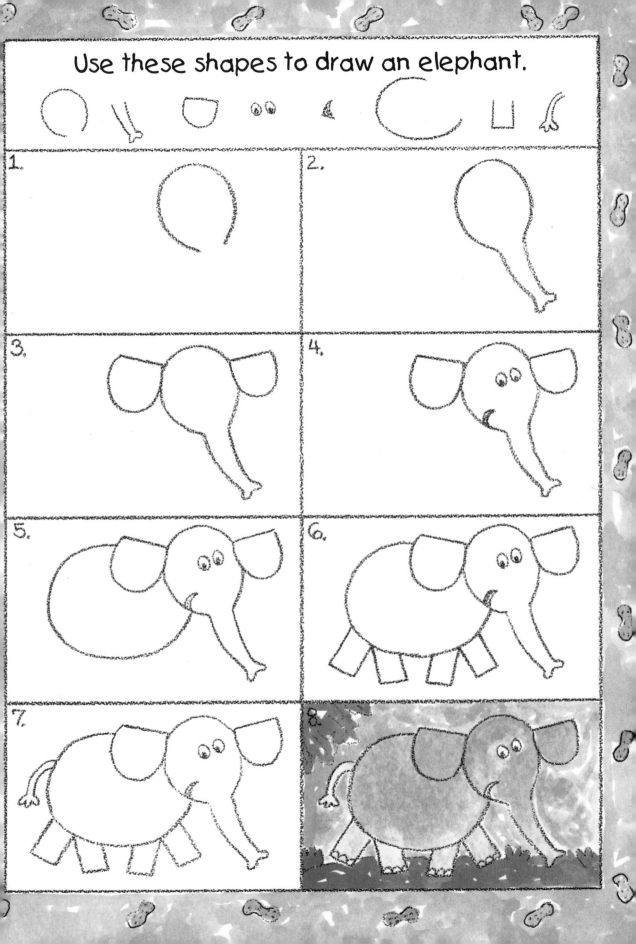

I can draw a giraffe
that is ten feet tall.

Use these shapes to draw a giraffe.

I can draw big animals,
like a polar bear . . .

Use these shapes to draw a polar bear.

or a moose.

Use these shapes to draw a moose.

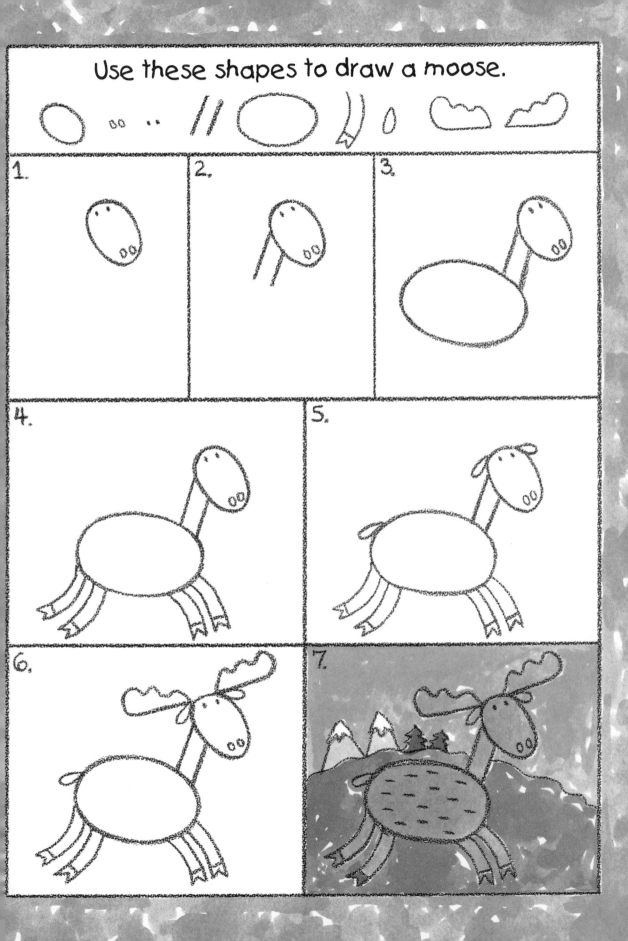

Use these shapes to draw a pig.

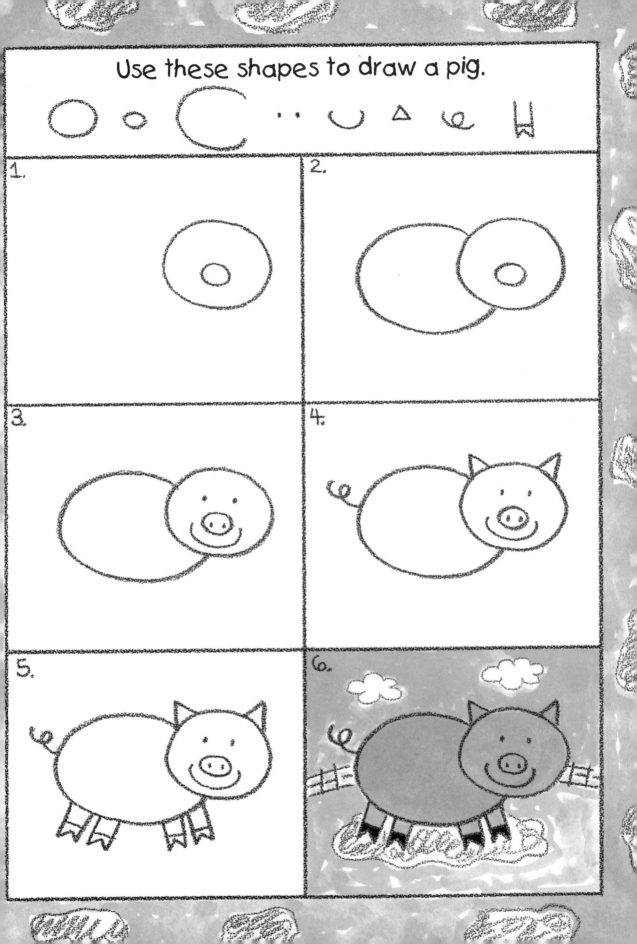

or a goose.

Use these shapes to draw a goose.

I can draw animals
that are happy or sad.

Show how your dog feels.

I can draw them for Mom.
I can draw them for Dad.

I can draw animals
that hop, slither, and run.
I like to draw.
Drawing is fun!

Draw silly animals.

And now that you
know what to do,
you can draw animals
and have fun, too!